THE WORLD OF NASCAR

Dale Earnhardt Jr.

By Jim Gigliotti

The Child's World
www.childsworld.com

Published in the United States of America by
The Child's World®
1980 Lookout Drive • Mankato, MN 56003-1705
800-599-READ • www.childsworld.com

ACKNOWLEDGMENTS

The Child's World®:
Mary Berendes, Publishing Director

Produced by Shoreline Publishing Group LLC
President / Editorial Director: James Buckley, Jr.
Designer: Tom Carling, carlingdesign.com
Assistant Editor: Jim Gigliotti

Photo Credits:
Cover: Getty Images (2)
Interior: AP/Wide World: 1, 2, 7, 9, 10, 13,
14, 15, 16, 18, 22, 28; Getty Images: 11, 17;
Reuters: 4, 21; Joe Robbins: 8, 25, 26.

**LIBRARY OF CONGRESS
CATALOGING-IN-PUBLICATION DATA**

Gigliotti, Jim.
  Dale Earnhardt Jr. / by Jim Gigliotti.
    p. cm. — (The world of NASCAR)
  Includes bibliographical references and index.
  ISBN 978-1-60253-074-4 (library bound : alk.
paper)
  1. Earnhardt, Dale, Jr.—Juvenile literature.
2. Automobile racing drivers—United States—
Biography—Juvenile literature. I. Title.
  GV1032.E19G53 2008
  796.72092—dc22
  [B]
                                    2007049076

Contents

[OPPOSITE]
*Dale Earnhardt's 2005 win at Chicago is
one of 17 in his career (through 2007).
Will a new team mean more trophies?*

"We'll Get Through This"

DALE EARNHARDT JR. RACED TOWARD THE END
of the Daytona 500 in February, 2001. The 26-year-old
was competing in the biggest **NASCAR** race for just the
second time in his young career. Michael Waltrip was the
only driver ahead of him. Dale Jr.'s dad, Dale Earnhardt
Sr., was just behind him in third place.

Dale Jr. put the pedal to the floor, but he couldn't
quite catch Waltrip and finished in second place. He
looked for his dad, but didn't see him. Soon, he and
NASCAR got the awful news: Dale Sr. had been killed on
the last lap in a shocking crash.

Dale Sr. was one of the most respected drivers in
NASCAR history. He also was one of the best. He won a
record-tying seven NASCAR championships.

The news stunned NASCAR fans. To NASCAR fans,
Dale Sr. was a legend. But Dale Jr. lost his father. "The
key to all my success is my dad," Dale Jr. once told
Sports Illustrated. "It's that simple. He taught me how to
drive, how to live with **integrity**, and how to be a man."

One week after his father's accident, Dale Jr. was
back on the track. He and his crew believed that is what
Dale Sr. would have wanted. "We'll get through this," Dale
Jr. said at the time. In many ways, he has gotten through
it. But in other ways, he's still got a way to go.

[OPPOSITE]
*Sad fans covered one
of Dale Earnhardt
Sr.'s cars with flowers
following his 2001
death at Daytona.*

A Family Affair

[OPPOSITE]
Dale Jr.'s grandfather Ralph (center car) was an early NASCAR pioneer.

ALMOST AS LONG AS THERE HAS BEEN NASCAR, there has been a famous Earnhardt racing in it. NASCAR was formed in 1948. In the 1950s and 1960s, Ralph Earnhardt was one of the best drivers. Ralph was Dale Jr.'s grandfather. Ralph is a member of the International Motorsports Hall of Fame. He was named one of the 50 greatest drivers in NASCAR history when the organization celebrated its 50-year anniversary in 1998. Ralph's son Dale Earnhardt Sr. also made the list. One day, maybe Dale Jr.'s name will be included among the best, too.

Dale Jr. never knew his grandfather. Ralph died of a heart attack at the age of 45 while working on his car the year before Dale Jr. was born. Dale Sr., however, instilled in his son a deep appreciation for the family's racing history. "I'm proud of my father and my grandfather and what they've done," Dale Jr. says.

Ralph Earnhardt won more than 350 NASCAR races of all different classes. In those days, however, stock-car racing was more of a **regional** sport enjoyed in

Numbers Game

There are some famous numbers in sports. Ted Williams wore uniform number 9 for baseball's Boston Red Sox. Hockey's Wayne Gretzky wore number 99. Basketball's Michael Jordan wore 23.

In NASCAR, famous driver Richard Petty (who was known as "The King") raced car number 43. Jeff Gordon, the most successful of the current stars, drives number 24. But the most famous number in NASCAR is 3. That number belonged to Dale Earnhardt Sr. When Dale Jr. began racing, his dad was still competing, so he had to find another number. He settled for number 8, the same number that his

grandfather, Ralph Earnhardt, raced under.

After Dale Sr.'s death, there was talk about Dale Jr. switching to No. 3. He knew he was already carrying on a family tradition with the No. 8, though. "My father did a lot for the number three," Dale Jr. says. "But the number eight had meaning for us, too."

the Southeast. Ralph generally raced close to his family's North Carolina home, often on Friday and Saturday nights. Many times, Ralph's son Dale went with his father to the track and helped him out in the garage at home. That fueled Dale's interest for racing. He wanted to be just like his dad.

In 1974, Dale Jr. was born. Soon, he also wanted to be like his dad. By the time Dale Jr. was old enough to hang out at the track, NASCAR was no longer just a regional sport. It was becoming a national **obsession**, and Dale Sr. was one of its most famous drivers. Racing usually took place on Sundays and in cities all over the

That's the famous "Man in Black," Dale Earnhardt Sr., out in front in the 1998 Daytona 500.

United States. That meant that Dale Sr. often had a plane to catch or a **sponsor** to call upon or an interview to do. "I was working and racing and going all the time," he said.

While Dale Jr. didn't get to hang out with his dad as much as he would have liked, it made the time they did have together all the more special. One month after his dad's fatal accident, Dale Jr. shared some of those memories in a column he wrote for NASCAR.com. "Since his death, these are the memories that help me through the hard times," Dale Jr. told his fans.

Once Dale Jr. joined his dad at NASCAR's top level, the two often met to share experiences.

Dale Jr. wrote about his dad teaching him how to ski when he was six years old. He wrote about a middle-of-the-night road trip when he got to tag along with his dad and some of his friends. Of course, there were racing memories, too, such as advice his father gave him when he first joined the NASCAR circuit.

Like any son, Dale Jr. didn't always understand or appreciate the advice. And like any son, he always strived for his father's approval. "It's like a never-ending process earning his respect," Dale Jr. once told the *Charlotte Observer*. "It's bottomless. . . . But it's something you always want."

Dale Sr.'s fans line up at his memorial museum in North Carolina.

Both Dale Sr. and Dale Jr. were born in North Carolina. Dale Jr. still has a home there. Dozens of NASCAR drivers live in the area around Charlotte, N.C.

3

Rising Star

Like his father and grandfather, Dale Jr. became a stock-car winner when he captured this 1998 Busch Series race.

WITH SUCH A FAMOUS RACING FATHER AND grandfather, it's no surprise that Dale Jr. soon got into racing, too. He started out as a kid by racing go-karts. Those are small, four-wheel racers with gasoline engines. Many NASCAR drivers got their start in go-karts. They allow kids to learn about racing without the danger of high-speed driving in bigger vehicles.

By the time he was 17, Dale Jr. knew he wanted to pursue racing for a living. So he and his half-brother, Kerry, teamed up to buy a **late-model** stock car. They began competing in the street stock division at the Concord, North Carolina, Speedway.

Dale Jr. quickly was on the fast track to success. By 1997, when he was only 22 years old, he already was competing regularly in NASCAR Busch Series (now called Nationwide Series) races. The Nationwide Series is one step down from the Sprint Cup Series, like the highest minor leagues in baseball. Nationwide Series cars are a bit lighter than, and not as powerful as, Sprint Cup cars.

Dale Jr. got his first rides at NASCAR's highest level during the late 1999 season. At that level, the cars are a bit faster and the races a bit longer than the Busch Series.

Dale Jr. took the Busch Series by storm. He placed 14th in his first event and needed only 16 starts before he recorded his first victory. The win came in the Coca-Cola 300 at Fort Worth, Texas, in April 1998. He won in true Earnhardt fashion, with a bold move to pass the leader on the last lap. Dale Sr. was on the radio during the race, helping to coach his son. "He used his head all day and ran a great race," Dale Sr. said afterward. "I couldn't be more proud of him."

There were many more chances for Dale Sr. to be proud. Dale Jr. went on to win six more races that year.

Family Feud

Dale Jr. and his brother Kerry made history when they joined their father in the same Nextel Cup race in 2000. In August that year, the three Earnhardts raced together in the Pepsi 400 at Michigan International Speedway.

Dad got the better of the boys. Dale Jr. qualified with the best time and sat on the **pole**, but finished 31st. Kerry spun out on the fifth lap and finished last. Dale Sr. started out near the back of the pack but finished sixth.

The only other time two brothers competed against their father was in 1960. That year, brothers Richard and Maurice Petty raced against their dad, Lee.

He placed among the top five finishers nine other times. By season's end, he edged Matt Kenseth for the Busch Series championship.

The next year was more of the same. Dale Jr. won six races and again was the Busch Series champion. He also got his feet wet in the Nextel Cup by racing in five events. He was ready to be a full-time driver in the Nextel Cup Series.

Way to go, son! Dale Sr. (left) greeted Dale Jr. after the younger racer won his first top-level race in 2000.

In April 2000, Dale Jr. won his first Nextel Cup race. It came almost two years to the day after he won his first Busch Series race, and it came at the same site. Dale Jr. won the DIRECTV 500 at the Texas Motor Speedway. Later, Dale Jr. added a victory in the Pontiac Excitement 400 at Richmond International Speedway.

Dale Jr.'s most memorable moment, though, came when he won The Winston at Charlotte in May. The Winston doesn't count in NASCAR's point standings. It's an all-star race. No **rookie** ever had won it before. That's not what made the win so special, though. What made it special was that Dale Jr.'s dad was there to share it with him. Dale Sr. joined his son in the winner's circle, and the two celebrated together. Dale Sr. didn't have a plane to catch or another race to go to, so "we jumped around and hollered and just made fools of ourselves," Dale Jr. says. "It was the happiest time I think I ever spent with my dad. I felt like I had really done something. . . . I knew Dad felt the same way."

Dale Jr. models one of his many hairstyles after winning the pole position at a 2000 race in Virginia.

4

Good Times, Bad Times

WHEN THE 2001 SEASON STARTED, DALE JR.

was determined to make his mark in the Nextel Cup Series (the series name was changed to the Sprint Cup in 2008). And what better way to start the year than with a good showing in the Daytona 500? Each NASCAR season begins with the Daytona 500. It is the most famous and most **prestigious** event on the schedule. It is often called the "Super Bowl of stock-car racing." Instead of being at the end of the season, though, it is at the beginning.

Dale Jr. finished a respectable 13th in his first Daytona 500 in 2000. He went on to have an excellent season that year, winning three races and finishing 16th in the overall standings. That wasn't good enough for him, though. He was disappointed that he was not the top rookie on the NASCAR circuit. That honor went to his friend Matt Kenseth, who finished 14th in the standings. So Dale Jr. entered the 2001 season determined to make it an even better year.

In the weeks before the 2001 Daytona 500, Dale Jr. had a recurring dream when he slept. It was **vivid**. "I'm pretty confident that I'm going to win the Daytona 500," he told the media a few days before the race, "because I've dreamed about it so much."

[OPPOSITE]
Son in front of dad: That's Dale Jr.'s red Chevy in front of Dale Sr.'s black one during the fateful 2001 Daytona 500.

Late in the race, Dale Jr. had a chance to make that dream come true. Unfortunately, it turned into a nightmare. Dale Jr. was running second, just behind Michael Waltrip and just ahead of Dale Sr. Dale Jr. and Waltrip raced for Dale Earnhardt, Inc., the racing team owned by the older driver. When it was obvious that Dale Sr. was not going to win the race, he decided to run interference for the two teammates. He drove so that no one could get past him and deny victory for either Waltrip or Dale Jr.

Full Circle

Like just about every NASCAR driver, Dale Earnhardt Sr. wanted to win the Daytona 500 more than any other race. Dale Sr. nearly won the event several times. Each time, though, something happened to keep him from crossing the finish line first. Finally, in 1998, on his 20th try, Dale Sr. won the Daytona 500 for the first and only time in his career. Dale Jr. won the historic race in just his fifth attempt in 2004. That year, he raced past Tony Stewart on the 181st lap of the 200-lap race and held on to win.

"Losing this race over and over, you could see it on his face," Dale Jr. said afterward when talking about his dad. "Inside of me, that started the desire to win this race."

Dale Jr.'s Daytona 500 win came three years after his dad was killed on the last lap of the same race. It's a sad connection that the site of Dale Jr.'s greatest sorrow also is the site of one of his greatest joys.

As it turned out, Waltrip held off Dale Jr. to win for the first time in his NASCAR career. The celebration in Victory Lane didn't last long, however. Word came quickly that Dale Sr. was hurt badly when his car slammed headfirst into the wall on the final turn. A short time later, NASCAR officials confirmed the worst: Dale Sr. had died.

After much soul-searching, Dale Jr. and his crew decided to race the following weekend at the Dura Lube 400 in Rockingham, North Carolina. "I'm sure he'd want us to keep going, and that's what we're going to do," Dale Jr. said. On the very first lap, Dale Jr. crashed. It was a horrifying moment for family and friends who were still

Meeting the press after the sad news at Daytona, Dale Jr. had to deal with emotions tougher than any last-lap duel in a race.

21

22

upset over Dale Sr.'s crash. Dale Jr. was all right, though. He walked away from the wreck uninjured. He vowed to try again the following week in Las Vegas.

Things went better at the UAW-DaimlerChrysler 400 in Las Vegas, but Dale Jr. still finished a distant 23rd. It was not until he returned to Daytona in July that he broke into the winner's circle again. He won the Pepsi 400 by holding off Waltrip on the final lap. Dale Jr. immediately dedicated the emotional victory to his dad. "He was with me tonight," he said after the race.

Dale Jr. says that returning to Daytona helped him deal with his father's death. It's no coincidence that his racing improved after that. He won two more times in 2001. By season's end, he had climbed to eighth place in the standings.

Family Ties

A father-and-son racing team is not that unusual in NASCAR. Many families have seen brothers, fathers, sons, and even sisters take part in races. Richard Petty, for instance, who won a record 200 races, was following his dad Lee, a former NASCAR champ. Richard's son Kyle is still racing today. In the 1950s, Tim, Fonty, and Bob Flock sometimes found themselves racing against their sister Ethel.

Other NASCAR families with two or more drivers include the Bodines, the Wallaces, the Waltrips, and the Jarretts. Bobby and Terry Labonte are the only brothers to each capture a NASCAR title.

5

A Name for Himself

DALE EARNHARDT SR. WAS ONE OF THE MOST
popular NASCAR drivers of all time. Without question,
Dale Jr. is the most popular of the current NASCAR
drivers. Fans voted him NASCAR's most popular driver for
the fifth consecutive time in 2007. And published reports
say that for every 10 dollars spent by fans on NASCAR
items, three dollars are for Dale Jr. gear.

Off the track, Dale Jr. is a celebrity. He has been
in many commercials for everything from soda to blue
jeans, appeared on talk shows, and acted in sitcoms and
movies. MTV and VH-1 have featured his interviews,
and his picture has been on the cover of more than
100 magazines. He counts music heavyweights such
as Kid Rock and Sheryl Crow among his friends. *People*
magazine, among others, put Dale Jr. on their lists of
interesting people. In 2007, he hosted an "Elvis Music

and Movies" series at Graceland, Elvis Presley's famous home in Memphis, Tennessee.

Such stardom has helped Dale Jr. build his own identity. For the younger Earnhardt, the comparisons between father and son have been **inevitable**. And for a long time, he was known simply as "Little E"—Dale Sr.'s kid.

On the track, though, Little E would like to be more like Big E. Dale Sr. won his first NASCAR championship

With racing skills and a famous name, Dale Jr. always draws a crowd at every race.

before he was 30 years old (he was 29 in 1980). Dale Jr. came close to matching that feat but fell short.

First, with the emotional roller coaster of the 2001 season behind him, he started strong in 2002. He suffered a **concussion** during an accident, however, and finished in 11th place. Then, at age 29 in 2003, he had a season that aimed for a real Earnhardt-to-Earnhardt dynasty. Dale Jr. won two races and was in the top five 21 times. He finished third overall in the points standings. "Junior's on his way to the championship," fellow driver Robby Gordon said at the time.

For the 2004 season, NASCAR started a new way of deciding the champion. After 26 races, the top 10 drivers in points would compete for the rest of the year in a special playoff called the "Chase for the Cup." Only a driver from among that final 10 could win the season championship. (Since then, NASCAR has changed the format to include the top 12 drivers in the standings.) Dale Jr. was in the hunt with a career-best six race wins. He was in the top 10 all year, even briefly spending time at number one. In the "Chase" races, though, Dale Jr. had engine troubles. He finished fifth overall.

A New Team

Dale Jr. made perhaps the biggest news of the 2007 NASCAR season off the track. It came when he announced that he was switching teams for 2008. It's always news when a driver changes teams. But when your name is Dale Earnhardt Jr. and you leave Dale Earnhardt Inc. (DEI) to join rival Hendrick Motorsports, well, that's front-page stuff.

"I wanted to find the team that was right for me as a person and where I could compete for championships," Dale Jr. said when explaining his decision.

Dale Jr. no longer felt that DEI was that place. DEI had been run by his stepmother Teresa since Dale Sr.'s death. But Dale Jr. was not making a serious run at a Nextel Cup title his final few seasons with DEI.

"The decision to leave DEI was the toughest I've ever had to make in my life," Dale Jr. wrote on his blog. "I love DEI and the people who work there."

Dale Sr. was the same age when he began driving for Richard Childress in 1984—a move that produced several championships. "I figure the best way for me to continue my father's legacy is to be competitive on a consistent basis," Dale Jr. wrote. "Earnhardt fans deserve wins and championships."

Most NASCAR experts figured Dale Jr.'s first season points title was just around the corner. Unfortunately, things haven't gone quite that well. He won only one race in 2005 and slumped to 19th in the standings—the lowest finish of his career. He won only one time again the next season, 2006. But after struggling much of the year, he came on strong at the end to qualify for the "Chase" and place fifth, as he did in 2003.

That was a nice finish, but it was not good enough for Dale Jr. So midway through the 2007 season, he decided that he was heading to a new team (Hendrick Motorsports) to pursue his dream of a Nextel Cup title (see box on page 27). He is a lot like his dad, after all. "I just want to win championships," he says. "That's all that really matters."

Dale's red No. 8 car was replaced in 2008 by this green-and-white No. 88 car (his new sponsor is an energy drink).

Dale Earnhardt Jr.

Time Line

1974 Dale Earnhardt Jr. born on October 10 in Kannapolis, NC

1996 Races in first Busch Series race

1998 Wins first Busch Series race and first season championship

1999 Drives in first Cup Series event; also wins second Busch title

2000 Wins the DIRECTV 500; competes against brother Kerry and father Dale Sr. in a Cup race in Michigan

2001 Wins the Pepsi 400 in his first race at Daytona following his father's death there

2004 Wins a career-best six races, including the Daytona 500, and finishes fifth overall on the season

2007 Announces that he will leave Dale Earnhardt Inc. at the end of the season and begin racing for Hendrick Motorsports in 2008

Career Stats

YEAR	WINS	TOP 5	CHAMPIONSHIP FINISH
2000	2	3	16
2001	3	9	8
2002	2	11	11
2003	2	13	3
2004	6	16	5
2005	1	7	19
2006	1	10	5
2007	0	7	16
Total	17	76	

Glossary

concussion   an injury, usually to the brain, that results from a blow to one's head

inevitable   impossible to avoid

integrity   sticking to one's beliefs

late-model   a term describing a car made in the past few years

NASCAR   the National Association for Stock Car Automobile Racing

obsession   an interest, job, or hobby that completely takes over a person's life

pole   the best starting position—the inside of the front row

prestigious   considered by many people to have great honor or importance

regional   relating to a particular area of the country

rookie   an athlete in his or her first sports season

sponsor   a company that pays an athlete or a team to promote its products

vivid   clear, strong, and lifelike

Find Out More

BOOKS

Dale Earnhardt: The Likable Intimidator
By Phil Barber
(The Child's World; Mankato, Minnesota) 2003
If you want to learn more about Dale Jr.'s dad, check out this book.

Dale Earnhardt Jr.: Born to Race
By Ken Garfield
(Enslow Publishers; Berkeley Heights, New Jersey) 2005
This book takes another look at Dale Jr.'s life.

Dale Earnhardt Jr.: People in the News
By Kevin Hillstrom
(Lucent Books; Chicago) 2008
An up-to-date look at the life of this talented NASCAR driver and sports celebrity.

Eyewitness NASCAR
By James Buckley Jr.
(DK Children; New York) 2005
This book teaches young readers all about stock-car racing, from NASCAR history to its greatest stars to the cars and the tracks on which they run.

Young Stars of NASCAR
By K. C. Kelley and Bob Woods
(Readers' Digest Children's Books, New York) 2005
Read about the early careers of Dale Jr. and many of his top rivals, including Tony Stewart, Ryan Newman, Jimmie Johnson, Matt Kenseth, and other top drivers.

WEB SITES

Visit our Web site for lots of links about Dale Earnhardt Jr. and NASCAR:
www.childsworld.com/links

Note to Parents, Teachers, and Librarians: We routinely check our Web links to make sure they're safe, active sites—so encourage your readers to check them out!

Index

ABOUT THE AUTHOR

Jim Gigliotti is a writer who lives in southern California with his wife and two children. A former editor with the National Football League's publishing division, he has written more than twenty books about sports and personalities, mostly for youngsters.